# *The Open Gate*

R. J. Keeler

Manor House

## Cataloguing Information

Keeler, Robert, J.

The Open Gate

(Poetry)

ISBN: 978-1-988058-74-0 (softcover)
ISBN: 978-1-988058-75-7 (hardcover)
I. Title

PS8631.R396P35 2021 C811'.6 C2020-906208-8

Copyright 2021-9-15 R. J. Keeler and Manor House Publishing Inc.

Published November 15, 2021
By Manor House Publishing Inc.
452 Cottingham Crescent, Ancaster,
Ontario, Canada, L9G 3V6
905-648-4797

First Edition / 130 pages
All Rights Reserved
Cover Design: Michael Davie, Manor House
Cover Art: MoreISO / iStock

*The Open Gate* / R. J. Keeler

To Dante, Angel, Apollo, Chief Frenchy, Elizabeth, Donna, Naomi, Jane, Jean, Sandy, Betty, Sean, Emilio, Dimitri, Justin, Nancy, Christie, Dr. Brooks, Lt. Peters, Dr. Sinclair, Dr. Weiss, Ron, The Mayo Clinic

# Contents

**Acknowledgements** 7

**First Part:** Love, et al. 11

The Open Gate 13
Slow Dancing with Action Figures 17
Maps, Serpents 18
Pump Down the Gas Pedal Hard 19
Corrosion and Its Many Uses 21
Dirty Magazines 22
After Jupiter Addresses Her Fate 23
She's Deaf in One Ear, I Mumble 25
Ruin as Gift, or The Equations of the Science of Love 26
Knot Theory: A Found Document with Light BDSM Added 27
Q-Boats 23
A Cha-Cha Is Just a Slow Mambo 34

**Second Part:** Death 35

How to Find True Happiness 37
Heading into Winter 39
Her Northern Sisters 40
Javert Is Evil—He Must Be Stopped, He Must Be Killed 41
Rune 43
Men of Yesterday 44
Sin-Eaters 45
The Razor's Edge 47
Sundae 49
Of My Province, a Dream 51
Of Dual Nature: Chernobyl, after a Pause 52
Divisions 55
My Mind Is Out to Kill Me 57

The Anthropologist Throws Up Her Hands 58
The Bodhisattva on the Ballard Bridge 61
At the Library of Souls 62

**Third Part:** The Natural World   63
Sun Rain Moon Tide 65
On Being Off Balance 66
Quality of Longing 67
The Growing Season 69
To Catch a Bird in Flight 71
Go Out into Far Fields of Glass and Flowers 72
Burrow 73
The Cloud Appreciation Society 74
Crows on a Wire 75
The Spider 76
Indigo 77
Rituals 81
The Spider Dips Its Legs in Water 79
Hive Mind 81
The King's Lands 83

**Fourth Part:** Science, Fun, Odds & Ends 85
Our Names Are Long 87
The Old-Age Home for Robots 88
The Clear Sound of the Bell 89
The Dinosaurs Went Extinct Because They
Didn't Have a Space Program 91
*Klaatu Barada Nikto* 92
On First Looking into Perelman's Proof of
Poincaré's Conjecture 93
No Dogs Allowed on the Beach 94
Ladder to Heaven 95
I Think of an Adverb that Watches the Sky 96
On First Trying to Grasp a Small Napkin on a
Café Table but Having to Repeat the Gesture
Five Times 97

Illusions of Water 99
A Harlequin 100
Rat Me Out 101

**Last Part:** Literature   103
Deception Pass 105
*Chinese Gastronomy* 107
The Point of Walking a Labyrinth 109
Alphabet 111
Amulet 113
Leverage 114
Blank Verses 115
Trivial 116
*Against the Fall of Night* 117
Both the Cross and Ecstasy of the Heart 118
Disfluencies 119
God Among the Insects 121
*Guerilla War,* The Libretto 122
Holystone 123
The Weld Is Always Stronger Than Steel   124
Listen 125

**Notes** 126

**About the Author** 129

## Acknowledgements

I would like to thank the editors of the following journals who first printed or selected these poems:

- "Alphabet" (as "Natural Selection"): *Saveas Writers'* International Writing Competition's Anthology (longlisted)
- "Chinese Gastronomy": World Food Day Special Call for Poetry, *Poetry X Hunger*
- "Crows on a Wire": *a fine line* (NZPS)
- "Go Out into Far Fields of Glass and Flowers": *Jung Journal: Culture and Psyche*
- "Heading into Winter": *La Piccioletta Barca* (shortlist)
- "Holystone": *Wingless Dreamer*, Daffodils Poetry Contest
- "Illusions of Water": *Voices Israel*
- "Javert Is Evil—He Must Be Stopped, He Must Be Killed": *IHRAF Publishes*
- "*Klaatu Barada Nikto*": *Voices Israel*
- "Knot Theory: A Found Document with Light BDSM Added": *The Poet's Billow*, 2019 Atlantis Award (semifinalist)
- "Maps, Serpents": *Voices Israel* 2020 Anthology

- "My Mind Is Out to Kill Me": *Proverse Poetry Prize*
- "On First Trying to Grasp a Small Napkin on a Café Table but Having to Repeat the Gesture Five Times": The New Zealand Poetry Society's *Poetry Anthology 2020*
- "Our Names Are Long": *Vashon Be Prepared*
- "Quality of Longing": *Saveas Writers'* International Writing Competition's Anthology
- "Ruin as Gift, or The Equations of the Science of Love": *The Peauxdunque Review*, Words and Music Writing Contest, (honorable mention)
- "She's Deaf in One Ear, I Mumble": *Willowdown Books* anthology, Human To Human
- "Sin Eaters": *Wingless Dreamer*, Daffodils Poetry Contest
- "The Cloud Appreciation Society": *Lummox Press*, Angela Consolo Mankiewicz Poetry Contest
- "The Growing Season ": *Two Thirds North*
- "On Being Off Balance": International Merit Award winner in the *Atlanta Review* 2021 International Poetry Competition.
- "The Weld is Always Stronger Than the Steel": *Soul-Making Keats Literary Competition*, Kathleen McClung "Beloved" Sonnet Prize (honorable mention)

- "To Catch a Bird in Flight": *The Midwest Quarterly*
- "Trivial": *Pif Magazine*
- Grateful acknowledgment to *Wikipedia* (https://www.wikipedia.org). Many of these poems were researched using their material.

The author wishes to thank Manor House Publishing and its founder, Michael B. Davie, for selecting this manuscript for publication.

Thanks also to a long line of teachers, mentors, and fellow students, including Guy Owen, Jim Heynen, Jana Harris, David Wagoner, David Whyte, Matt Briggs, Belle Randall, Richard Kenney, Linda Bierds, Christianne Balk, Jan Wallace, Jane Hirshfield, Nikolai Popov, Susan Lynch, and most especially Heather McHugh.

This work inspired in part by the late poet John Lawrence Ashbery, who wished his work to be accessible to as many people as possible and not to be a private dialogue with himself.

*The Open Gate* / R. J. Keeler

# First Part: Love, et al.

# The Open Gate

a normal morning.
nothing much of any significance here, apart
from the open gate.
just a garden outside that appears to be hovering
upwards.
the garden plants grow without major supervision; no
need to cheerlead them to rise up, bloom;
    their agenda—nothing short of a long, happy
life: blossoming, opening wide under a noon sky.

then the sun glides inside the yawning house; the
floor rugs steam up with solidness.
alongside the crisp lawn and tended flowers, laughter
from the front porch and open door;
    dogs frantically barking after kids flying around,
towing stuffed bears and puppets.
if there were radians crossing this arbitrary curve of
heaven, they would lend grace.
a few steps away, on a polished wood table inside the
door, *The Golden Notebook*
    open to its last chapter, a counterweight to
whatever's going on inside.

the screaming kids, pursued wildly by the family dog,
slide and trip over rugs, tumble harmlessly;
    nothing here seems under any measure of
control, not even gravity or vitals, although neither
    is disorder the rule.

## *The Open Gate* / R. J. Keeler

the full story unfolds in small segments, like some
blow-up paper party toy.
three, even four, generations breathe and move in this
large, old house of creaking floors and
    sides.


the senior women make the path here, but delicately,
quietly, out of sight, like roots outside;
    those roots' work now nigh—they cannot be
shallow, nor can they be tender,
    though a reed becomes stronger by being
hollow—something about carrying less weight.
then in comes music, Mendelssohn or cello, yet it
seems to fit the hour.
the entire oeuvre—garden, women, wives, children,
book, music—lateral, but enough;
    the unruliness, and messiness, a form of
containment from outside, from underground.


hard luck for the kids inside, the dog finally caught
the furry rabbit and decimated its innards.
it feels like there's something here for everybody,
perhaps even theatrical;
    the tableau's like a birthmark, *is* a birthmark, that
goes on and on to a fine edge.
backstage, nothing happens except for ecstasy of
eggplants and celery out in the garden.
the whole house suddenly becomes lyrical and
unbecalmed, tossed-up and whole,
    a drumbeat of angled happiness, a house full of
screaming kids and barking dogs.


how the screams and barks give the
grandmothers a sense of peace and future.

## *The Open Gate* / R. J. Keeler

the women are content; one goes out into the sunny
garden, has no longing nor fear.
were this field to be obliterated at that instant, she
would do nothing different but enjoy the voices.
a white tornado springs up just inside the door's
threshold, toys flung everywhere.

the garden, the rugs, the old women, the young
wives, the happy barking dog;
    what more could be desired, what added
ingredient—one atom
    of dirt that feeds the garden that feeds the women
and their babies and yes, the dog?

heat rising, one measure to push the way forward; the
heat from the garden just phenomenal.
if the sun were suddenly to disappear, the earth
would settle into fifths, one for each daughter.
in the kitchen, the gang gets busy folding thick rolls
and baking bread, dripping the frosting;
    in an hour or two this will all be on a cooling
rack on the wide table, everyone circled, waiting.
when the eldest leans in and lifts a buttery flake of
browned bread, each young girl follows suit.

whispers move down through realms of light, into
rows of corn and salads.
time is being counted—everyone's heartbeat slows
then slows; why so normal?
a progress in the lower gardens of the household—
young women rebel in spirit.
wisps of contentment ripple across the lawn and up
onto loose, channeled rugs;

    nothing can come between these women and
their fortunate earth.

around the busy ring of hallways, a hot vortex rides
the children's shoulders.
they see only today and a small slice of tomorrow;
this, their just moment to breathe, shine.

        at close of day, what's not solitary to that
still place?

oftentimes, in the small of night, young girls in sleep
dream only of wholeness and mothers.
in rooms, in private desks, in locked drawers, wives'
and girls' letters drift to bold sentiments;
    if unrolled and read, they point to feelings of
love and need, of solace and peace.

softness sprinkles down over their warmth.
young womanhood will be outlived and forgotten;
young women will grow into strong maturity,
    whereupon the reign of life commences again,
ongoing.
the strength of the hour will bleed away, be
distributed without need or cause,
    neither sad nor constrictive, just cool skin, just
wildfire inside.

## Slow Dancing with Action Figures

And music bathes a sprung fir floor
where duos twirl in camo or Kevlar.
On a felted, stained bandstand of lore
horns, tentacles, eyestalks, and tails:
hard bodies bound with excess scales.

Cute alien girl burps lime vodka,
cuts a dreary routine out of Kafka;
her teeth and fins grow intifadas.
Slow left turn synchs, arpeggios rappel;
ballroom spotlight glitters across babel.

Drool-wipers scuttle between fixed sets.
Weapons checked, but not lethal threats;
no fun at this maximum-security downbeat.
Who pairs with whom, or safe in deep dips?
Megalodon recommits his vows to shrimps.

Nancy Pearl in a strapless, low-cut hugs
a wall, takes a chance on a robot hybrid,
while blood-thirsty Godzilla cuts a rug.
*Hell of a time*, grunts He-Man, a low-brow,
leading his date in a three-step waltz combo.

## Maps, Serpents

Children need the maps they rarely get
to get to where now is.

When I was five, I lay
in blackened, silent bedrooms
to watch a bright moon
pour its light through open,
barred windows.

Two years later, I walked
toward home on many dark,
cricketless nights, straining
to hear in rasping silence.

Nowadays, acquaintances discuss
how boring T-bills are, then go throw
themselves from Cessnas
at ten thousand feet.

Sometimes, there are only
old, torn fragments
to guide us—somewhere,
we must all land.

We know ourselves
to be blessedly lucky
if an ancient artist drew,
among heightened waves
and spouting steams, four
or five ugly, coiled serpents
in our map's distant
tattered corners.

*The Open Gate* / R. J. Keeler

# Pump Down the Gas Pedal Hard

Silvery light interplays.
Snow-covered pines rise up like brush-marks.

Horses kicking and stirring, nipping rumps;
they are in the day of now, not the day of tomorrow
      or of yesterday.

Every kind of love spreads across the range of lands;
garlands of summer flowers will be offered to
      passersby and to circus caravans.

What the hell, the Great Mother Bear watches over
all of life, so pump down the gas pedal hard, drive
that old pickup truck right up to the bar door.

--------------------------

God, how we hoped for reliefs and salvations. What
      we envisioned
was so colored by noir recollections of drab and hull.

Go on then, own up to your mistakes—we all make
      them. Show your humanity
as a bright wave coming up and over—our history of
      defeat is not the scope of life.

Go on, close your book, stop reading, go out and do
      good works;
over the ages, none of the great moral philosophers
      ever got that right.

And, if you're lucky enough to find hidden treasure

> in the back yard, give it all up.
> The Wise One, who is ever around, will reach out
> > shortly to replenish.

---

All the hellishness in *The Garden of Earthly Delights*
> suddenly turns humble;
happiness is not the end of the day, because dimness
> must also be accounted for.

But when the slim hand reaches back to grab the
> latecomer— the same hand
that moves the crystalline light ahead—

then the edge of the sun's limbs graze and shift
> behind soft curtains;
what human eyes can't presently see, contextual
> hearts already know.

## Corrosion and Its Many Uses

Iron sharpens iron, corrosion is such a lovely game,
the handmaiden of desire, like eternal spring.

But language never corrodes; a word if once
is then forever; it wipes memories away,
whitewashes
sacraments of office. Nothing's ever constant

or even at the center of everything, whereas hate is
so powerful, its goodness fails every nuance.

While all around, everyone's trying to sell something,
or prepare as martyr for the downing lash.

Yet, in this world of feeling
love can corrode love—now, Captain Blood

struts to the bow and thrusts his rapier out into the
        dim fog ahead.
His thrusts are like steel on stone; his every crime
        unpunished.

## Dirty Magazines

This long con opens out to sheaves of quartz and
uncut tourmaline, but there's always the browning
leaf among the bright rose and tulip. Those bodies—
mischievous wonders; furred casings roiled, frothy.

Touch the love-dirty mags: plant-based, teeming with
centermusk. The saucy tragedy of the commons is not
about community or futile hope; like flesh's stunning
manifestations, then plowed like succulents, not just

porn. Elmer Gantry rose to sing and plead, "Come to
Jesus"; his crowd's instinct, to fall down onto knees
and palpate their psalms. Like far-off snowpacks,
titillating in their new winter clothes, photos drift

across our view, half-naked or visibly aroused.
An example of how catholically a sad brain
works: too much of anything a sin, but too
little of anything a sin. Bottoms, chests, thighs,

confined to four corners of dog-eared pages; a sleazy
picture—acquired taste, or much too banal to deserve
our comment? We went where wind took us, to the
fourteen corners of earth—like a compass to

north, caught what we hardly knew, and
hung on. What fleshy worlds have I not
yet touched? What foreign lands have
I not yet visited? Who here
is not my true
mistress?

## After Jupiter Addresses Her Fate

What does a priest ever do for me—
for any of us? I will build a small ark
for our reindeer, to save them,
even though they care not for us,
or even for Jupiter. Quite miniature,
they will populate dumb earth, build a
space program, send probes to gas giants,
ask forgiveness for sins and visitations.

Even though they want not to be saved,
they are progeny for our future; alone,
we will never survive the oncoming
extinctions.

Jupiter, Jupiter, you used to be our god,
but now you are mortal, like us. Your sad
love infected by a virus of congruence.
Tomorrow, the end of an old parade starts—
early flowers in the late snow, such a gentle
touch to hold. Tonight, snow moon, bone
moon, hunter moon—only moon. We are
fractured so much we shatter; then life
goes on. Belief in Jesus the only way,
some would say.

*The Open Gate* / R. J. Keeler

A pebble is poised at the lip of a cliff;
if it moves, it falls, mitigating earth's early
catastrophes. We will come closer
to Jupiter; she will shield us from all harm.
But once the obscure dentist
drills a hole through her ether,
she becomes like a weaseled gambler: zero
cards to play, just a hand full of jokers. ■

Jupiter has lovely breasts; I will go to her
room at night and play with them. Beautiful oaks
grow in her vagina; red oaks will flower and bud,
drop leaves, and I will cut them down. Proceed
to open new, official consulates in Brazil,
in Argentina, since Jupiter can now take care
of herself. Go find true refuge for your
endless inadequacies, and bless philistines,
for they contribute nothing to naïve diaries. ■

## She's Deaf in One Ear, I Mumble

Holy slick bananas, what good is yelling, just
wakes up snoring cats. Perhaps there's still time to
begin to learn ASL. But even if, she'd have to get on
board too—surely never happen. Tired, worn Navy
signal flags a better option:

▪ Kilo: *I wish to communicate with you.*

▪ India: *Coming alongside.*

▪ X-ray: *Stop carrying out your intentions and watch for my signals.*

▪ Uniform: *You are running into danger.*

▪ Delta (after three or four G&Ts): *I am maneuvering with difficulty; keep clear.*

▪ Mike: *My vessel is stopped; making no way* (two more).

▪ Zulu: *I require a tug.*

I gave it my best.

# Ruin as Gift, or The Equations of the Science of Love

Newton's First Law of Romance:
> In every romantic frame of reference, each soul acts on uncountable others, and is, in turn, acted on by them.

Newton's Second Law of Romance:
> In every romantic frame of reference, each force of idle touch feels permanently appreciated and reappreciated.

Newton's Third Law of Romance:
> Every messy breakup propels souls into another brute heart's arms.

Gauss's Law of Romantic Magnetism:
> There are no singular romances; romantic lines of force never begin nor end, not cleanly.

Maxwell–Faraday's Law of Fleshy Attraction:
> Work per unit of soul required to move around a closed dance floor equals the rate of change of unimpeded lust along the outer walls.

Einstein's Mass–Energy Equivalences:
> Any attempt to search for some foreign heart of nature will dissolve every other soul's magical underpinnings of trust.

*The Open Gate* / R. J. Keeler

# Knot Theory: A Found Document with Light BDSM Added

[There are] tame versus wild knots.
—Crowell and Fox, *Introduction to Knot Theory*

*Knots:* The most numerous group who uses knots is made up of the millions of ordinary men and women who use knots about the house—in the kitchen, in the garden, on holidays or camping trips, for a great variety of purposes. . . .

*Overhand Coil:* Once you acquire the knack, it's very easy to tie. Untying it is simple too, provided you pull on the right parts. If you don't, the. . .may become snarled.

*Figure Eight, or Flemish, Knot:* Best choice for a general-purpose stopper knot. It also remains easy to untie, even when pulled tight, and doesn't injure. . . .

*Stevedore's Knot:* Good for keeping a knot from pulling. . . . Commonly used on ropes running through. . .fairly large openings. An extra turn makes the knot even larger. . . .

*Overhand Loop:* Keep in mind it's difficult to untie and can damage. . .especially if pulled extremely tight.

*Monkey's Fist:* A decorative way to add weight to [an] end. . . . By itself, the knot probably won't be heavy enough to make that much difference. . . . But if you insert a small round stone in the center, the knot will have an adequate heft to it.

*Heaving Line Knot:* While not as classy as the Monkey's Fist, the Heaving Line Knot is much faster. . . . This knot also makes a first-class fender to protect. . .from damage.

*Mathew Walker's Knot:* While laid-up ropes are slowly losing ground to braided ones, it still pays to know at least one good [one]. The Mathew Walker Knot is one of the finest. It's good-looking, quite strong, and fiendishly difficult. . . . After you tie the knot, twist the strands back together and whip the end of the rope to finish.

*Hitches:* Hitches are among the most common and useful knots because they are used to tie ropes onto other objects such as poles [and] rings. . . . When deciding which hitch to tie, you will have to take into consideration the load that will be placed on the line (heavy or light; shifting or stationary) as well as how long the rope will hold the load (5 minutes or overnight). The easier hitches. . .may be a better choice if you need to undo them often or quickly.

*Cow Hitch:* A fast, easy way to attach a line to a post or ring. It's quite adequate when tied on the bight, and both ends are under tension.

*Half Hitch:* An Overhand Knot tied around. . .a stake or a pole. It's never used alone as it slips under load.

*Midshipman's Hitch:* This hitch is very useful for [f]rigging. . .because it can slide along the standing part to take up slack. If tied tightly, the knot will hold its position, keeping. . .taut.

*Permanent Guy Lines:* When properly tensioned, guy lines help to keep the pole upright.

*Timber Hitch:* For towing or hoisting a log or other cylindrical object, it's hard to beat. . . . It holds tenaciously when. . .under tension, yet it won't jam or become difficult. . . . This hitch is often used in conjunction with a Half Hitch or two, which helps keep whatever you're towing pointed in the right direction.

*Clove Hitch (also, Peg Knot):* Unfortunately, this isn't a particularly secure knot, especially if the tension on it is intermittent and shifts position. . . . Always consider this knot a temporary solution.

*Mooring Hitch:* A more secure means of fastening a line to a pole. You do, however, need to have access to the pole's end.

*Trucker's Hitch:* Especially useful for tying cargo to the bed. . .because it allows you to clinch down the load and keep tension on the rope as you finish. . . . It's worth learning just so you can feel smug in the home center parking lot. . . .

*Halyard Hitch:* When it's all drawn up, it presents a very neat appearance. The combination of aesthetics and security makes the knot an excellent choice for such tasks as. . .control.

*Catspaw Hitch:* For heavy lifting, it should be tied in the middle, leaving both ends free to carry the load. The knot won't jam, and it comes. . .instantly when removed from the hook.

*Swing Hitch:* Unlike the Clove Hitch, the Swing Hitch is very secure. Even when it's subjected to a shifting load, [it] maintains its grip. . . . This makes it a prime candidate for hanging a rope swing because it won't slip or chafe. . . .

*Sliding Ring Hitch (also, Italian or Friction Hitch):* This knot isn't supposed to hold fast. Rather, it's supposed to slide freely. . .when the line is slack, but jam up tight under tension.

*Surgeon's Knot:* This knot is somewhat ungainly because of its asymmetrical construction and may require a little coaxing to draw up well.

*Bowline:* The Bowline is the one to learn because it has so many uses. You should be sure to draw it up snugly, especially when it's tied. . .stiff. . . . It's a fun knot to teach to young [omitted], because you can perform a "story" as you perform the steps necessary to tie it.

*Double Bowline:* The knot makes an excellent sling work seat. [It] leaves your hands free to. . .manipulate tools when. . .aloft.

*Running Knots:* If you need the rope back, it pays to have a plan for getting to the knot later to untie it.

*Carrick Bend:* Popular among [those] who work with heavy lines because it always draws up correctly under load.

*Double Becket Hitch:* Although whaling is in decline, it seems a shame to do away with all that's associated with it.

*True-Lovers Bend:* It's hard to beat the [true-lovers bend].

*Sheepshank Knot:* This knot holds tenaciously—as long as it's under tension. But once the line goes slack, the Sheepshank will all but fall apart.

*Blood Knot:* Gets its name from its resemblance to the knot used at the tip of a cat o' nine tails. Fortunately, it's use isn't that macabre. It's a good gentle knot. . . .

*Grinner Knot:* Who can help but think about good times when tying the Grinner Knot.
<u>Lashings:</u> These knots can be used to build significant structures. Lashings are also handy for projects on a tamer scale.

*Parallel Lashing:* Parallel lashing is used to join poles side by side. . .to make a longer pole.

*Rope Care:* It is foolish to buy good rope and then treat it carelessly. . . . Avoid kinks in the line. . . . It is

generally not necessary to oil or lubricate rope. . . .
Check rope often for deterioration, opening the lay. .
.for inspection. A smooth taper will result in a more
efficient splice.

*Small Stuff:* Small stuff is generally considered to be
3/16- to1/2-inch diameter. . . . It is favored. . .for
light-duty and decorative projects.

## Q-Boats

Deception such a lovely game, but lonely,
so rain rains undeceived, not even clever.
The worm of desire's at front, as bitter feint
after feint turns love on its back, for love.

The falling rain—simple sultry water;
the lonely mating dance of phantom peacocks;
not deceptions but rather, cleverness.
A pitcher plant's deceiving only second to life
itself, while Cylons evoke the human form;

deception leaves no watermark, whereas
the clever girl finds solidarity
with shallow-draft ships and banked fires.
Cunning's radius this magnificent:
a lovely, lonely tune, old and worn.

Someone, something always deceives the heart;
what's the manifest, the unlife, force?

## A Cha-Cha Is Just a Slow Mambo

The dance floor seems endless—an enormity,
        incomparable;
but where's that caress in the dance of life: a simple
        smile, a wave, a glance.
The curve of love turns around and touches its own
        hem. And then time shifts;
the feet know what to do, unlike fumbling mind.

Suddenly there's a herd on the floor; it seems safer
        than all-aloneness.
Dancing's so tribal; coax dance-music out of its
        cave—don't ever suborn it.
Look, strong music can't fool anyone. Steps are like
        rules, but then
everything's a rule, someplace not too sweet.

Rites determine outcomes; if a dance can make you
        do something, shouldn't it?
Mambo sounds like a sour ruse, from a dark jungle of
        continents. One person on a dance floor—
bravery. Fifty—heaven on earth.

Dance, pick a mate who jives best, latch on for life.

# Second Part: Death

*The Open Gate* / R. J. Keeler

*The Open Gate* / R. J. Keeler

## How to Find True Happiness

There is a point and a line through each life
like a lengthwise curl of wave—a vector
advancing, foaming, then breaking
wherever bottoms shoal up.

Lightning now forks up and down, jaggedly
around some comely girl's silhouette,
like a large-gauge railroad track off to somewhere
only to fall back down into the nearest station.

And suddenly, some misshapen heart beats true,
but still ugly, like the white bark of a young tree
whose outermost spirit swells up into fifth octaves.
Look, one sights everywhere a whelped-up mess,

and rats in branches of verdant trees concur. Jove,
Hera, lay out our shoes, my lexicons;
calculate our disasters, send us them quickly.
Advise our Books of Samuel to lift higher,

to rain songs down upon painted canyons. Light
from a far star drifts across a life and changes
it, clears it to thrum. Like wild red horses in snow,
any bitterness or envy defeats our montage heart.

---

Deep inside our lives lie positive happenstances;
they can bless and fix us, lift us up to tops of hills.
And around every fine head we'll wrap ribbons;
they'll free us to refined travels, to recolor air

*The Open Gate* / R. J. Keeler

into scintillated wavelengths. Thus,
our human heart remains an existential heart,
a metaphoric heart—an old paradigm's secret heart—
each one a sapling in a forest of billions; each,

like a sapling with lightness and air, is elusive,
evades the darkness, hides. The universe
is steadily flying apart into nothingness;
there is no indication it will ever reunite.

## Heading into Winter

*Take off your old coat, put on the new,*
the old song sings, but winter's not
a friendly herald come to bless
our feast, to save our tired skin.

*Aphelion*—the way-tired term, of looming
dearth of brighter light. This-here multi-
verse, created to show us how to live;
it wraps around, like a monkey's tail,
all the dirt that makes us lasting human,
*bitter* human.

Which sun's our antidote to bail us out;
we're not so brilliant as may imagine—
*The deepest trench we could imagine?*
And chess it seems is neither art nor fun,
nor science. So stand below and watch
yourself navigate that frozen higher wire.

Don't look down—really don't—nothing
underneath except our rotten, testy sun,
whose very inclines to righteous truth
drag your feeling-senses like a vacuum.

*The Open Gate* / R. J. Keeler

## Her Northern Sisters
— Mt. Rainier and Cascadia of Northern America

The thirteen sit in pomp, a silent line
strung across a cold arc of urgency.
Sisters, they hold collective breaths;
they pray, they sigh for continuity.
Along that old, red-fired crescent
they deign to whisper loud, north

and south. Undemur, all thirteen
siblings arc-welded into Cascadia's
deep strata, into impossible time;
this was never their promised land.
That parabolic set of kindred souls;
closer to a spiteful dozen—the larger,

far distant. But every sister's frozen—
what may they ever do, what's lost
each day just by standing there?
Were it that they might pace about,
not just hang syncopated breaths
on high, or wave their lacy hankies up

and down the crescent line, bow a noise,
or occasionally shiver deep. Some were
married once before, but now—no dashing
companions. So, where's their hot, promised
change of life—their deep-down tremblings?
They all command a boring, minor slice

of near-eternal time. But no hard line will
be held indefinitely, nor hard. Wait it out
forever—impossible! And neither is shrinking.

## Javert Is Evil—He Must Be Stopped, He Must Be Killed
—Victor Hugo, *Les Misérables*

*Javert, why do you pursue me so?*
In his heart, Javert knows he's right,
right up to the hour he doesn't.

What does it matter why?
A twig breaks or a twig bends—simple.

But time goes on apace, as always.
Roosters out in the pasture accept an uprising sun—
        a new day to crow.

Hell if anyone anywhere knows what or how they
        actually think;
like using teaspoons to count oceans with no spillage.

*What an artist dies in me!* he says.
Even this uneasy universe seems to be conflicted.

*Javert, if you ask, God could touch your brow*
        *to remove a suffering.*
That blue-and-white flower next to me as I sat in
prayer this morning was unconflicted.

A dog's soul either exists or not—no secular debate.
Your best child has died; then, after all, it did not, so
        returned scarred but whole.

*The Open Gate* / R. J. Keeler

The supple bough bends with the wind.
Even continents slide and occasionally kick up
    unhappily.

Is an *I love you* static or conditional, or neither?
Light of goodness burns Valjean's eyes.

## Rune

A black mirror then curved around;
I saw the light of my life and indulged
her broad, honest face—untrammeled.
We'd picked *Perthu*, a formidable rune.

A blood-red bud, rose of distant death—
a girl walking down a sunny sidewalk
hears a dim footstep at her rear. Panic!
Hit again by that hard imagined stythe.

Bar girls in skimpy shorties ply a trade
with dregs and fools. House rules always
seem to favor baccarat and craps. Soon,
holes in pockets, cold shock of water.

Life's security—ours, theirs—always faint;
wearily the red fox accepts a wan détente.

## Men of Yesterday

A Denisovan, hurrying to return
to his home-cave, now vacant
of children, women, and dogs.
He's interrupted by dim nature's
exactness; his bundle of fire sticks
scattered along his uphill trail,
thus come to naught; a cat left
its crimson tale along winter snow.

Bitter clouds massed and boxed,
north and south of just no more
happiness—of nothing more. Moss
spread along the cold north side
of the last heart since transpired;
weak claret marks the permafrost's
thaw that the cat paused to lick.

Empty fields afterward are
administered, statutory, but not
hampered. That former day
like a block of black stone, a day
which may return, but must.

# Sin-Eaters

*The art and science of sin-eating*

i. So like a hummingbird, sins are colorful, vibrant
. . . everlasting.
And, now that you've died, bring me all your unrequited sins—
although, please, first let go of any bluster and confidence;
this is one time your dirty tricks won't work.

ii. How long since your last sincere confession? Do recall, Sir,
Madam—delicate sins alight daily on your once-naked soul,
so best be sure your now-deadness looks totally spick-and-span.
*Just in case*, my professional motto, *just in case*.

iii. First, I motion a crust of old, moldy bread across your whole
now-cold body; at finale, I chew and swallow the entire crust.
Thereafter, raise that cold hand, pass me a handful of now-
useless farthings—see, I never ask much for doing my job well.

*The sin-eaters' credo*

i. After decades of sin-eating, sin-eaters do become somewhat
incendiary. So, please, do not ask what I do for fun; this is a
profession, not a hobby.

ii. But yes, of course, this job involves sacrifice.
    At first, it's a heady job; but soon, reality comes
    by, tips its hat.

iii. A conscious sin-eater will even eat unconscious
    sins.
    But can a sin-eater eat her own sins? No.

iv. My own sins? They will not be visited on my
    children.
    In fact, a sin-eater may never herself sin.

## The Razor's Edge
—W. Somerset Maugham, 1944

What a race of giants!
Came from where—and went to where?
Their ancient, once-sharpened implement, now left
behind, stands upended against desert winds.

Their whetstones and leather long ago dulled or lost;
sere razor worried all-about by gray-stained mottles
and endless pockmarks from past ceremony;

vanquished nicks, flecked blood from that lost race.
Each season a torrid winter sun evacuates every
gray ledge-shadow of those long-exterminated eyes.

The upright, dull blade's fatal scars of unmeasured
intercourse; shocking wear-and-tears
could be the consequence of live skinning parties,

wars or battles, amputations away from anesthesia;
why else extensive cracks or bitter striations
that divide its crosswise planes

into remarkables very near its sunlit edges?
Visible too, meager hieroglyphs that may, eras past,
be of machining inside a long-dead cottage's

heated forges; the maker and sons or daughters
obtained pleasure in a red, raw-smoking ingot
by deep impress of their ancient forge's credentials.

This razor's edge—now still and dull—dominates a
        cloudy back-plain.
Once, a razor served its masters well; now,
unfaithfully it connives to wipe out an old, bitter well
of longing, lust, and hate majestic; sated,

undefended, pristine inside its torn-and-worn image.

## Sundae

i.
The counter clerk does not have any
   great quantity of this flavor,
certainly not under the category "Pistachio."

So, I ask: when the red circumstantial
   rays of a starfish
slide up over a mollusk's shell,

and its tips join and lock
   together underneath, mustn't some
amount of this—what?—be created
   inside the mollusk's casing?

Does the mollusk, then, just go on quietly
   feeding? For it, that's filtering seawater
as the starfish's central, spiny
   mouth commences to bore and grind?

Wholly nonchalant? Up to
   what point?—even, perhaps, just
as the starfish starts to suck
   out finally the soft, chunky, white
cream it's excavated?

ii.
Perhaps the dzeren (zenu) lends a better example:
What is mirrored by the dzeren's locked eyes
   as it dances to the lioness's quick, hard pants
close on its outward flank? Or outlined through
   its wild, springing leaps?

*The Open Gate* / R. J. Keeler

Or later, just before the lioness
   starts to lap the bright
pool of hot cherry syrup—was some
   of this substance to be found there?

iii.
A new species runs the ground today:
gladiators who bludgeon
   with fat words; who,
when the crowd roars
   for the finale, turn
and together butcher their own
   sponsors. A species not
content to just kill, instead
maims for its trade
and arrogant pleasure.

iv.
So I say: last night, when the process
   server's unexpected hand
rapped on my steel front door, and rapped more,
   I understood that which—ordinarily—
can't be measured in scoops, nor
   in hand-packed pints:
it's too solvent, too lethal.

Personally, last night, it
   made my guts unstring and
descend, heavy.
   I crouched in my wool socks
and stared unseen out the peephole. I want to
   know—what explains fear but
a desperate want to live one more hour?

## Of My Province, a Dream

The moon rose and set, I saw, along its singular axis;
day-by-day I walked under, saw *la lumière deliverée*.
And chanced a low, wild valley, that sparkling river;
its river-light led my clan out of low, dusty hills.

Cold was high in the heavens, in the river's beds;
my wife and two daughters smoked fish and roots.
Evenings, we tossed dry sticks or hollowed bones.
Oft my dreams changed; our dogs barked and fled.

One night, I strode up hills seeking moon's brilliance.
In a wink, dust rose down-valley, river twinkled.
Fast as shadow, a dust cloud came like red catarrh.
I ran but not far; my family and it found consilience

Right after earth tilted came its screeching thunder.
Ribbons of animal magma plowed us asunder.

## Of Dual Nature: Chernobyl, after a Pause

The aim of the rules and safety systems: to minimize the risk to the point where a reasonable individual would conclude they are. . . .

What's *de minimis* risk value, and whether it has been achieved by the nuclear industry remains a subject of bitter. . . .

Through a combination of operator errors, coupled with the failure of an important valve to operate. . . .

But a common thread was that the human element was a more important factor in safe operation than had been heretofore. . . .

Table 9: Values for the maximum permissible concentration (MPC) of certain radionuclides

| Isotope | Critical organ | mBq in body |
|---|---|---|
| Tritium | bone | $7.4(10^{-3})$ |
| Strontium-90* | thyroid | $1.5(10^{-6})$ |
|  | bone | $1.5(10^{-7})$ |
| Iodine-131 |  | $1.8(10^{-6})$ |
|  | thyroid | $2.6(10^{-8})$ |
| Cesium-137 | thyroid | $1.1(10^{-6})$ |
| Radium-226*** | kidney | $7.4(10^{-8})$ |
|  | bone | $3.7(10^{-8})$ |
| Uranium | thyroid | $7.4(10^{-8})$ |
|  | kidney | $1.8(10^{-9})$ |
| Plutonium-239 | bone | $1.5(10^{-8})$ |

^ Indicates exponentiation.
*MPC in drinking water: $3.7(10^{-9})$ micro Bq/liter.
***MPC in drinking water: $3.7(10^{-10})$ micro Bq/liter.

At this point, I was stuck. I just could not go on and on any further writing about depressing topics like strontium-90 and iodine-131. I decided to think about histopathology, to see where that led.

Actually, I began instead to imagine the "traditional cultures of the Arctic." Did you know that "the taiga form of reindeer husbandry occurs on a much smaller scale because of the impossibility of supervising large herds in a forest environment. The reindeer themselves are of a larger stature and can be ridden and used as pack animals"? Now, this is quite important, because "taiga dwellers would build pyramidal or conical tents covered with birch bark (in western regions) or larch bark (in the east)."

The following renders this especially interesting: "Traditional religious belief and practice throughout the Eurasian north was shamanistic in form (indeed, the term *shaman* derives of Evenk derivation). According to the shamanistic worldview, the cosmos were divided into many layers, and the shaman, helped or hindered by various spirits, is thought to be able to travel in trance between them and, in so doing, to achieve an integration essential both to the health of individuals and to the well-being of the community."

Finally, the clincher: "Vigorous ethnopolitical organizations have been established which have fought effectively to reverse the stigma that once was attached to Sami identity, to secure respect for their language and cultural traditions, and to assert their rights—on the basis of prior occupancy—to land and water. Materially, the Sami can enjoy the benefits, in terms of raised living standards, of their citizenship of relatively affluent welfare states; however, the Chernobyl nuclear accident of 1986, which spread radioactive material over much of northwestern Lapland, dealt a blow from which the reindeer economy may be slow to recover."

## Divisions
—For Francis Farmer

Cygnus the Swan fell below the edge of the flat prairie. Dawn approached. Five men entered the women's sleeping lodge, lifted and carried the girl, a girl of thirteen summers, still in her sleeping furs, outside. The older women inside lay frozen.

Since childhood, the young girl, orphaned, strange to her clan, had been a whisperer; and later on, one who stared out at distance. Now, the five men quelled the girl, mounted up, and cantered eastward out of camp. At midday, they came to higher ground, then, beyond, a ring of quaking aspen around a small stream. Here they left her; one older man turned to say, *We must protect our heritage, it has guided us ever since Black Eagle created this tribe.* A second turned: *You scolded us many times, shamed us, demanding, We must return, We must go back. . . .*

An early fall day; on that high ground above the plains, heat lightning scattered a warm rain. The young girl, alone now; comforted by the Wise One above. That past spring, as she sat on the prairie grass alongside the horse camp, each time Hawk or Crow or Eagle crossed softly overhead she would upbraid the gathered clan—*We must return, We must go back. . . .*

Each day of that hot summer, women brought her food and drink, but the men, especially the older council men, would carve their path on the beaten grass well away from her, staring not at all at her.

The waning moon was mid-height when a clan of women—one of many out on the prairie that night that had ridden east—rode up into the high glen and gathered her. They returned her to their lodge and fed her and gave her drink. Afterwards, she stayed silent; but now, forever.

## My Mind Is Out to Kill Me

I will ask it delicately to reconsider.

*Would you care for a dark chocolate?* I will ask.
*Perhaps you'll ask me to spank your bottom?* I ask.

I have many classics in my library; perhaps you'd
    care to browse a few?
Like *How to Be a Double Agent for Dummies*—a
    book even I might understand.

I could utilize a clever disguise—surely my mind
    would never find out.
There are times like now when I think I'm talking to
    myself in falsetto.

Could I sneak up on you when you're dozing and
give you a good hard thwack?
    Could I trick you into going to a car-
crushing junkyard and getting you involved?

Would my mind ever let me use it as a punti in my
    glassblowing class?
Perhaps I could put you into the hot slumping-oven
    for a few hours.

I am going to go in and disarm my mind, take away
    all its lethal weapons.
*Mind, any chance we could change places?* I'll ask.

For $50,000 I could hire a pro to do a hit job on my
    mind—but oh . . . wait.

## The Anthropologist Throws Up Her Hands

She wonders exactly how to break out of her habits
        and her formal trainings.
She observes that all her hillsides are alive and
        shedding their warm water;
how is it that even a faint baby flea has some foreign
        consciousness?
This instant there stands in front of her a small
twirling black hole, or else a skittering black cat.
Or a crane, not known to song, but graceful and tall,
        knitted of snow and wax.

She waits patiently to head out into the bush to do
research, to capture natives on daguerreotypes.
Pigs and chickens root in the dirt street; an
accomplished piano player cum *futbol* goalie
sings in the roadside bar. There, startled out of deep
slumber by a faint buzzing, by fright, disgust, or
        surprise—
what does or doesn't she see out in the open field of
        her own victorious thoughts?

Thus, her confidence builds apiece while papayas
        feed the guacamayas and bird
spiders become hungry for dinner. The tight-lipped
anthropologist, trained by fire in jungles
way below the equator, may begin to project her
mind up onto the plantain stalks and leaves
so that she may be the first to understand what
consciousness manufactures out of notes and
        warbles.

*The Open Gate* / R. J. Keeler

For some reason she has birds on her mind.
Thousands of feathers litter thoughts
but deny her a careful, traditional, process to collect
        unimpeached data or facts
for subsequent publication in her own backwater
        literary journals.
Now she returns to the hills so very covered.

The vise heads across her dumb ears pulsate every
week or two, at their apogee her thinking clears,
she recalls that her sisters and brothers also went out
        into the bush but evaporated, overnight;
or maybe she becomes aware they stayed home to
        play darts for lunch money.
In time, her cannibals re-direct to those old teenage
        drawings she had illuminated and scored
for her eventual funerals among tribes of red howlers.
        She believes them consequential.

What do these monkeys want of her, they follow her
        from tree to tree, howling her name, or else.
*Come clean*, they muster, *and we'll forgive you, and
        then you can sit and eat a papaya
and be content with your puny, topical life.*

She thinks how to trick them into performing for her
        so that she may finally get tenure.
These provincial bureaucrats, all they care about is
        lux.

But then bells strike noon and while the corrugating
        sun is at peak, she gathers her gear
and stalks down into the hot valley to finish her
        research work.

She needs to water the birds down for the night but
        the pipes seem to have broken.

*The Open Gate* / R. J. Keeler

## The Bodhisattva on the Ballard Bridge

Lucy walked across the channel
each day in June for lunch.
The air was full of sea; she'd journaled
*Good Intelligence*.

The slightly unbound Werner ladder,
at twenty-eight feet,
whipped her into *Light-Maker*;
her brow beheld the street.

Sadness and deep compassion, or anger
at a mindless masoner's truck?
Her seventh bhūmi's *Gone Afar*
at a ladder swung athwart;

how wide it snapped our body's eyes.

## At the Library of Souls

Why keep souls in a library when they need to fly?
Debased and rotten, folded into unequal parts
like an old tree or grove or leaned portal,
all alike conscripted beyond usefulness of rays,
unevenly contradicted, famished—all quite dead.
Pressed like foreign flowers within pages of
    illuminati
a lone soul can forage for six days without food,
but may stop to rest eyes on friendly dog-eared
    pages.
Souls instruct themselves on printed words to soothe;
to perch, souls' winged tongues must flutter in
    concert.

Break the spine of any book of trudging souls
and fission of a nature instantly strikes—
souls' silklike neckerchiefs twine and dance.
Though they may no longer thirst or feel,
what might they want? On holidays like Mole Day,

give them a ribboned box—empty, like space.
And unlike pages in books, souls may embrace
or even intertwine like a tangled ball of string.
Still, they can fly swing, or square dance to banjos.

Souls misclassified or buried in corners struggle.
The stacks lift up in unison and shirk their weight;
    the unseen will be seen
long after their great passage into the Vast Between.
Ah, but they can all be checked out again for future
    use
in superior lives. There will be no fines or overdues.

# Third Part: The Natural World

*The Open Gate* / R. J. Keeler

## Sun Rain Moon Tide

Four deities assemble overhead,
watching, hopeful, alert, and tense.
Bridged hands across huge cumulus;
when the winds and tides strain at us,
where should we stand, or tend?

Four deities direct our myth—vain
paths we construct lives by:
invisible, atomized, tie-dyed mists,
yellow or purple, that abide.
Arise the wandering unsane,

arise Sun, Rain, Moon, Tide—
four aesthetic deities, quite eccentric.
If we turn our back, they'll hex us,
break us apart, then come back
to sweep off, to clean off, ill minds.

Synesthesia and the like make
cloud and tide to raise their hips
and undercut the shore's myths.
Thrumping hearts move the needle.
The four deities, never opaque.

## On Being Off Balance

The southmost bearing pear tree
subverts balance as strictly ordained.
Crows bully all the ripened fruit,
sweat bees cave the broken lanterns—
dazzling and proud, that fallen talent.

Chance itself needs no balance,
shifts back and forth between.
If chance itself levied a truce—
if Yang consumed, swallowed, Yin—
it'd turn a muddled gray.

*Nature abhors a vacuum*, we say,
but seem to worship the wrong god.
Seeing imbalance, we all reflect—
maybe love's the higher nature,
maybe love's a spicier roe.

Rise up, seize the fragile toehold,
seize whatever's leveled out.
Poise conscripts again and again,
vibrancy's the solid option.
Be not prepared for everything.

May the mighty Gates of Ishtar buckle,
may spice plague your every season.

## Quality of Longing

Yesterday, today, tomorrow—these are not for the
       faint of heart.
That old triad of longing unfolds, on and on, will
       never end;
that longing's from back before you were ever born.
Glance down an old, enduring line of mothers, the
       seat of all—
two million years that lineage revived your current
       state of heart,
repaired a middle tear in your whole cloth, window
       for futures.

High overhead, the lone eagle eyes its repose with
care, while earth
       settles into furrows, smooths and loves its
own slipperiness.
The rain has fallen as it has always fallen, but its
       moisture is not wet;
Gaia has arranged this sideshow for time longer than
       dirt.
Look, nature's ambivalent, doesn't care for
       matriarchy, or for elephants.
Win or lose, there's always another galaxy to move
       to, someone else an
       eternal mother.

Ursa the Bear fornicates without regard for her
       strange emotions.
Her lineage lives on forever, one star at a time, like a
       perfect being.

## *The Open Gate* / R. J. Keeler

Her regal mothers bridge back into tropical
    savannahs; then,
after the Star of the Big returns, fold up their old
    hearts
    to make passage back to future heavens.
Presently, an old woman comes out to sweep up the
    mess and tidy.

*The Open Gate* / R. J. Keeler

# The Growing Season

A small, young deer trots by me and it, too, is
        Buddha.
These days are like adventures in love and
        babysitting,
the miles below mahogany, dark.
On the veranda, many standing blooms.
On the limestone hearth, many pictures of weddings.
Then nature takes its course—everyone's life
        becomes
wacko messy like a fairy tale in pallid watercolors.

Now, all these many rivers run into inlands.
Now, we're all whispering into flames.
The ground underneath seems razed—
where comes that arterial that falls to some flat sea?
There, compendiums of black sails and white sails:
which one life, which one death?
Remarking on ordinary blackness—it's not just a lack
        of roses
or a narrow path between elms or stones on the dirt or
        clouds above.
It's moral weakness at the heart of roots and
        branches.

Now, it comes to pass: fear signals too strong a verb
while over there—salt on the floor, the old soft-shoe.
Alternatives seem dim, no way out except through
some weep hole in a narrow canyon. Just like
an old building, some Masonic temple,
or vine or turtle that carries the world on its back.

Once in a while the good fairy does come out on top
    enough to count.
The dykes are still holding back the sea,
air still plentiful about to lift a kite,
water enough for fledgling corn and melons.
*Give it up, enjoy life*, a sexton preaches, *who are you
    saving it for?*
The growing season means there's one that's not.

## To Catch a Bird in Flight

A bolt to jet a bird aloft
whose wings were fins to hold
a foreign water above or underneath;
and light was free for all who chose—
the air devoted to fallen, blackened
rock—and time was free and given.

A small movement, adjusted easily,
a fluttering sideways or even inwards,
on a minute, on an open ground;
there was no time and finished
late or not at all—wings churning
a last conceit before uplifting.

Upward, some very sliver of light;
its rays streak along longer wings,
their hollow cantilevers admitting
less than heartbeats to lift aloft.

Wanderings and murmurations fix flight—
and us with heavy arms glued to earth, but birds grip
air and rise to sun or star, compress the ether.
Adroit to feel height, to stun the pull of dirt,
and flash to hope and brilliance, like locust
hordes come out of buried, drying earth.
What hand reached quick to bend
its path of flight?

A bird thinks less of air than grass of dirt,
yet bird's no portraiture of lightness.
It owns its space, and lacks every
evil motive except to be aloft.

## Go Out into Far Fields of Glass and Flowers

This is like doing something you really don't want to
        do,
but you do it anyway because you have to, or want to.
It's like tossing hot juju on the waters in order to
        scold.
It's like holding a sick daughter's hand for an
        afternoon's
arc across land; go, weave your small spells into the
        water.


When you march an army across a bridge, break step;
resonance, a fancy word—music can crack a steel
        span,
even a softer chime can embody a reader's daily hope
not to skim across her open epistle, but to dig in—
        know
that any target of her misbehaviors can make a wild,
        wilder.


Go out into far fields of glass and flowers and sit,
        you.
Open your hands wide, breathe in downy snow; open
wide your illuminated codex. In there, fellow
        pilgrims,
you'll enjoy seeds of hope and power; petals will
        open
to your silent wish, and no one will be becalmed,
        ever.

# Burrow

Burrow as artifact: a secret place, deep.
The warrens brim with life.
A secret place; only few live here.
Hidden sometimes in the open,
    a sweet place, safe, no longer an island.
Each colony lives apart in its own burrow;
    each colony lives or dies on its own.

A song of loss, the strongest song or tune.
Loss is such a dirty word, it can't hurt to say it twice.
There is a song in the air, always in the air, elaborate
    and colorful.
Somedays the only thing to do is to ply the universe
    with song.
Birds above and in the hair; they make a happy
    racket, no kestrels overhead.

April is breeding time,
    grass is softer after a long rain.
Form is crucial—a burrow is a cul-de-sac: a nest, a
    green lawn and pool.
Only us there, but exclusion defends.
This is about hiding things away.

## The Cloud Appreciation Society

Clouds, mainly gray or white, nothing but wet
wind and frilly metaphors; they present
random shapes—like Rorschach tests
to probe our id—then slide away
to conspire.

Weighing tons not ounces, enjoying neither
spine nor inner strength, nor brains nor hearts;
sophisticated, meek—clouds never take orders.
Rogue cabals guide them, push them across outer
worlds, into boiling Venuses.

Clouds innocently look to dive underground
but resurface out of hot springs or lava cones,
or take on tormented, snakelike, and zebra shapes.

May I be allowed to live in my own cloud forever
until my waters boil away, then, make my way
out beyond Saturn's unmanageable rings,

or start over at home as a copper tea kettle
with no painful attachments, or live
in some damp mist, never needing parlors

full of goshawks
and caterpillars, their cocoons
unraveling into wisps.

## Crows on a Wire

Four crows on a wire,
properly separated,
all wearing black masks.

## The Spider

the creative who hunts,
seeks out darkness or sturdy jungle leaves,
finds no two reasonable points too far apart
   to connect;
ploddingly re-spins a web carried away by some
   much larger beast
unless the beast is captured.

## Indigo

Color of old, coldest ice beneath
new-fallen snow, fathoms deep,
has brought every purple berry
to smash onto a fine bone plate,
to stain floral china darkest blue.

A plant—unlike the rest—its smallish
rough green pod to burst
along a slack, medial seam,
to gape anatomical splay.

Cuff intense, this purple light
streams across a dyer's hand,
explodes a native virgin sheet,
stamps blue tints on warp and weft;
a fictive handshake not undone.

Until a war begins, the dye is ours.
So covet trades that keep the flower
violet-pink and meters-tall; milk
its leaves, cook an inky paste,
send to ancient clothing looms
who'll blue impress a lass's blouse.

A violent-blue assaults the hurt;
the stain's not the stain for long.

Love for the tiny blue bush, love
for the stain that clots and covers,
for the rift that rectifies the blaze,
and lastly, for the root that bears.

# The Spider Dips Its Legs in Water

The spider stands
on the cup's foreign lip,
wondering down
at the stormy ocean
close by, underneath.

Pure phenomenology,
both king and queen,
architect and engineer;
its mitochondrial mother
watched Jesus walk
across waters of Galilee.
Peter tells of a miracle;
why not it too?

The spider's eyes
witness a reconciling
of forbidden scripture:
a graving dock aside water,
a mirror pocked by sun,
a king tide to compensate,
and a reflection—a monster.

Tipsy from nectar,
its feminine on display,
the language of nature
turns to crown it hero.
But the spider on the lip
asserts
it's just
all about
philosophy.

# Rituals

Burdened by high priests, they bind lesser
and greater gods to our sides; whatever they
may promise, will they favor our fate,
or turn a flat back to us?

The wisdom of an old lead elk graces her
herd's reckoned arc. Raptors and
scavengers circle in wait, sniff, gauge
possibilities. What does she remember—of
what use is she? She's had her run. But
soon, she turns half-back, tosses her life's
learnings astern. These pass to daughters,
even to sons, in turn. Abler rivals arise,
overtake; her finish comes unwelcomed.

The old elk, now long dead, still holds on to
her charmed carapace. We all unfold small,
hushed hands and receive there her soft,
formal glass—molten spice, a promiscuous
chant. That wise elk's ancient elixir floods
across certain vast oceans of nature. Sour
marsh grass arises, rewards small
grasshoppers that still do hearty work—
useful around late blooms in alpine
meadows.

While, up at terrible altitudes, occasionally
at 40 degrees below zero, greylag geese thrum
down their winter migration, dowsing for
their greener path, for their watery ring—
solid earth, engraved yet foreign—for a
leveling of hearts, for a press to open onto
a rarer faith.

*The Open Gate* / R. J. Keeler

Rituals—well-worn, animal-kind handiworks.
Burnished or unburnished, they seal us in
their rosiness. Flip a fair coin, choose which
door to open. Most everyone knows the
small bite of real fear comes between their
charms and a life.

Look at the rising green grass of the
Southern Cross, little distorted from the
Paleolithic; so, rooted in that rise, night
upon night, we grasp at fragmentations.

## Hive Mind

i. Here is hive-mind's secret:

    it folds, then unfolds, then
    folds back onto itself again
    like a heaving shark gill
    far out of serious water.

ii. Every single hive-mind

    swims like an evil hunter-
    shark, cutting a murky path
    through heavy water.

iii. A hive-mind's drone bee's

    wiggle-waggle dance only
    may confirm that its hive
    will not perish at coming
    winter's prevarications—
    even enable it to faintly
    predict winter, the bad
    it might be.

iv. But that naïve bee's slinky

    prognostics may also
    fumble when dispensing
    such dire divinations.

v.    So, who's best to shine

       numberless bee-paths
       onto brutal winter's final,
       chancy, ever-best salvation:
       a modern, enlightened, but
       lone, brain; or some silly, but
       interconnected, hive-mind?

## The King's Lands

Midnight—everything at an all-stop.
Ascend the towers of the cathedral,
from there see over the king's lands.
Someday these will all be yours.

Hear the language of the dinosaurs.
Their words become like wild flame;
flame becomes dirt, dirt compresses
to song, but song blossoms to flame.

Capture the fun of our eternal moments.
Encourage generations of unruly children
who, in turn, will own the songs and flame,
and topple the king's towers down to dirt.

Confetti clouds the thin, rare air;
all kings are forced to abjure.
Then the terminator's shadow
may lay out, artfully, safe harbors.

Subterraneans alight the tower buttress.
Dirt so good, it sings a rabid song—
like a smart dog, it chases its forlorn tail.
What's left to speak about?

*The Open Gate* / R. J. Keeler

# Fourth Part: Science, Fun, Odds & Ends

*The Open Gate* / R. J. Keeler

*The Open Gate* / R. J. Keeler

## Our Names Are Long

Our names are long, but what of it—
who cares if they laze and droop
and bump along? If names were short—
like drops of water, all most alike—
there'd be a sea, a tide, a flood of them.

Long names straighten doubt out:
so far as I know, I've only met five
(or six) *OzymandiasRumpelstiltskin*s.
But even one of those (I knew her
well) employed as middle initial
*OldKinderhookTheThird*.

Lo, what a terrible misfortune—
to be named (oh, sad!) *Ann Sow*
or (most vile!) *Vi Ng*. There must be
seven or eight—maybe ten—jillion
parents come to claim those children after school.

Me, I'd pick a better name: the six
million names of beetles, repeated
a google times a google times.
This pins the named down most well—
to maybe two or three assorted folks,
but still. . . .

There's only one name among
a jillion envied will ever *really* pin
a person down uniquely, as should
be. Like the texture of our mobile
tongues, like the color of our toes,
by heart we all know this one—me.

# The Old-Age Home for Robots

Caged in tight rows, like flocks of
grocery carts waiting to be shoved
off by busy after-work shoppers.

Little that may be called human.
Feelings, thoughts—absent, not even
a faint, low instinct. Many, though, sport
proud, surprisingly bright, patinas:

incandescent greens, metallic blues.
But for the lowest—the mud hogs,
the pole skinners—drab's the uniform.

They are done.
None will ever leave here in a working piece.
None will ever serve.

Out in far time, may they strut and clank.

# The Clear Sound of the Bell

The clear sound of the bell lingered. Waxing and waning, it floated outward to intertwine with a bird's harsh cries. Low in the background was surf. A fourth thing—like a hammer, perhaps an ax—then joined in. The entire medley wavered softer and louder.

After a few minutes the ax's staccato glided to regularity. For just a moment, bell and bird and ax and surf coincided. Then, the ax's staccato slowed and fell out of rhythm. The surf's repeated low churning continued. The bell—akin to a finger run lightly around a wet glass's rim—and bird provided counterpoint.

Far away, the animal sat in darkness and listened. For a while, its ears strained into the night's quiet, but nothing else was forthcoming. In this blackness it listened most intently—sat still on cold, grainy soil, its long, tapered tail curled alongside a left hind leg, the tip wrapped, looped back underneath a slack belly and poked out over the right leg.

After a little time, off to the left and halfway up an imagined horizon, the animal faintly sensed something—a rich, repeated ringing. It seemed singular, with a peculiar trill shimmering back and forth, each pulse lasting no more than five heartbeats.

The animal peered farther into the night; it sensed a second beat, but this one most unsympathetic; heavy with force and with strange threat simmering in it—

most unlike the somewhat friendlier, continual, soft, trilling sound. This second beat, a chunka-chunka-chunka, arose a quadrant to the right and lower down. It was pointedly, clearly disturbing to the animal's three cochlear ears, each peaked up out of its back along its spine, one behind the other.

After a while, slowly and dimly, the blue fog cleared; up to the north, a dim, red sun reappeared.

*The Open Gate* / R. J. Keeler

# The Dinosaurs Went Extinct Because They Didn't Have a Space Program

Woden's day, in a year so long ago
        there were not yet years to be remarked.
We think it may have been at day, we think even a
        clear sky above,
but if at night, then the ingress was visible, sudden.

Fish jumping all over the place, moon high
        above eastern horizon, bright in daylight.
Then the eastern window opened; eyes uplifted to the
        sky,
then the arrival of that black, dark cloud.

Out beyond, there was never any noise, not even so
        much as silence;
silence is a song of absence—of something, not of
        nothing.
If it had been one hour earlier or later
we ourselves would not be here; it was either

them or us. It must have
        looked like magic,
like some valanced game of chance, or a desperate
        pinball.
But this was not imaginary—everyone withered;

someday they will all be covered with clay
                              then baked solid.
Everyone was already dead
        before they knew it.

## *Klaatu Barada Nikto*
—*The Day the Earth Stood Still*, 1951

Inchoate as a heavy hunk of steel, Gort,
the hairy robot, lurks and waits.
*Shall I save my master, or send Earth to its fate—
or both*, its alien synapses snap and tickle out.

The answer not long in arriving: Klaatu,
who came to teach our planet to reverse
from certain ruin, is tortured and traversed.
But Helen speaks a phrase to halt the coup.

*The Open Gate* / R. J. Keeler

# On First Looking into Perelman's Proof of Poincaré's Conjecture

Curly and Grisha—shape-shifters, gave no ground.
Poincaré and Trickster Coyote, both happy at end.
Curly, Custer's Crow scout, slinked down a gulley;
Perelman's battle? Ricci tensors and heat entropy.

But everything changes, everything is connected;
entropy rules topological worlds. That being said,
given sufficient time *all* immaterials shift shape.
Perelman's proof excised unseemly horns; Sioux

women cut Custer's brave heart out, gnawed it apart.
A slack genius by ten, Perelman taught at Courant,
but Custer cast at the bottom of West Point's class.

Both were tactical, strategic, and inclined to rashness.
Curley's blanket, a topological surface employed to
        disguise;
Perelman reflowed Poincaré's 3-sphere down to
        rational size.

## No Dogs Allowed on the Beach

No dogs allowed on the beach, as if
the beach cared; they only snap at flies.
Also, no ferries on land
No signs on top of waves
No crosses up in clouds
No cliffs. And no cryptographic
       names carved into their foot:
*Marina*
*DVS in __ Liz!*
No discoloration of the seaweed
No Tampaxes buried in wet sand
No inverted flags
No teaching a girl how to skip flat rocks four times
No tautological proofs
No natural selection
No downed telegraph wires
No sprung clamshells jammed into tree nooks
No *Tamp axes regrets*
No conceding three moves before checkmate
No benches erected
       *In Memory of*
       *Harold Sondheim 1990*
No failed antiskid, antilock braking systems
No other German engineering marvels
No writing just on odd-numbered pages (. . . on even-numbered
       for left-handers)
No rearview mirrors
No tears in rain gear
No Dogs Allowed on the Beach (RCW 10.3B.11)
Nothing after 1919
No key rings

## Ladder to Heaven

By tradition, a ladder to Heaven provides many,
many rungs to climb. But were those rungs,
tragically, to number less, where might one end?
Golly, dangling high above firmaments of earth
and water, and far below those Pearly Gates.

If, *au contraire*, a ladder sports too many rungs—
bunches, tons, excesses—one might just blindly
climb past cloudy realms of dogs and gods,
past eternal pastures, to ascend where?
Wow, amazing—His very crowded attic!

So if you chance to grace His attic, please note
every detail and content. Then, if you ever again
touch ground, please confirm all rumors: chests
of Parvaim's bitter gold? A charred, desert bush
or two? Abraham's busted, low-rider chariot?

And some eighteen drafts of stony, musty tablets—
and not one of them with benefit of spell-check?

## I Think of an Adverb that Watches the Sky

Bleakly, out on some forsaken Scottish moor
Calmly—good, but not during a Katrina-like
  hurricane
Cheerfully—no, much too personified
Clearly: a day at the beach sunning, encouraging your
  melanoma
Continually: if you are a SETI radio telescope
Deeply: if you are the SETI telescope looking out at
  Vega in the film *Contact*
Deliberately, if you are an ancient Phoenician sailor
  trying to find your way to Knossos
Elegantly, if your first name should be Albert
Gladly, if you are looking for a sign from the gods on
  how to survive local dynastic overthrows
Highly, if you happen to be flying a U-2 on a secret
  spy mission over Cuba.
Jubilantly, if you are a *Connecticut Yankee in King
  Arthur's Court* at 12:03 p.m. in 528 A.D.
Mechanically, as an average streetlamp photocell
Mightily, if you are Atlas holding up the sky
Never would be good, but not true
Not, if you're a Cayman Trough hydrothermal worm
Regularly; mostly true
Upbeatedly, true for Category 5 cyclones in your
  backyard
Vacantly? Yes, if you were Metope, punished by her
  father Echetus
Warmly, if you are a $CO_2$ molecule
Wetly, well, during a Rangoon monsoon
Wistfully, if you happen to be Icarus in Auden's
  "Musée des Beaux Arts"

*The Open Gate* / R. J. Keeler

# On First Trying to Grasp a Small Napkin on a Café Table but Having to Repeat the Gesture Five Times

Straining to hold and fight, galactic winds, generally
> headed west,
push it out of reach;
while in front of me, out of skirting dust clouds, the
> human brain
does not agree.
A yawning crevasse, like thighs between the two
> parties, alongside
the wicker basket
of happiness—trying to touch the hem of the sacred
> object. How would
you change things
to where there's an upbend in the risk-return curves?

Jade and pearl, ruby, all the precious stones spill like
> some kiloparsecs
from my hand
out across and around the table. Heat rises,
> malignancy in the
fingernails, sweet and caring,
low down. Everyone enjoys their dreary suppositions,
> with slippery
slopes ahead
and on all sides leading down into the maw. Swamp
> monsters lunge
and bite at my outstretched hand.

The task of knowing begins with solitude; you can't
> know what you
can't touch.

## The Open Gate / R. J. Keeler

Even touching, there seems a need to reinterpret what
> is missing—this

just the tip of the spear,

the absent force. No good to come out of this time of
> drastics.

The air turns warm between the paper and the hand.
> The strangest

flowers, *Clever-as-Always*, open up.

There are no feelings around the café's table—a
> fetishizing party.

The air, stolen.

What seems to be before the eye may be a fair mirage
> instead.

Is this another casualty of love?

Overturned tables and apples strewn across the floor
> are real.

## Illusions of Water

Safer than chlorine and even smoother;
what else do you need if you have water?

Sometimes it may be disagreeable but . . .
$H_2O$'s symmetry—such an all-time burden!

For those trebled love affairs, now ice-cold,
neither weep nor fear, you ghost fish souls.

Water acts wiser now and can't walk away;
its essence depicts a now-darkling plain

where a fleeting bird holds a high C.
Paper-scissors-rock looks invincible, solid,

but wiser water devours the paper, rusts
metal, dissolves hard rock in centuries.

Interesting that water rose very quickly
and silently, overtopping during the day

the posings of Florentines selling scenarios
on the middle deck of the Ponte Vecchio.

I like illusions, because they do work—
so, come closer, and look closely;

does all this water look calm? It's not.
Anyone astute can tell what is part

truth and what's not. Accidentally deluging
auras—less mess than subtly sidestepping?

# A Harlequin

This instrument of resonance, an iron
law of what's already there—The Fool.
Onstage, the harlequin whispers
to draw unruly audiences closer.

A noisy backfire, then a sight gag,
a pirouette, a wooden sword smacked
hard across Grimaldi's costumed butt—
crude as spit and twice as deafening.

*Agronomy's the answer,* he jokes. *I piss
on proper and décor; I'm paid to get
the audience to gasp and shriek and faint.*
(Red lightning forks, settles into sheaves.)

His anti-Hippocratic oath? A tuba
for his throat, a kazoo up his rear.

# Rat Me Out

Frack this holy ground
it can bear no weight;
no constitution at hand
to assuage our guilt.

But use a bigger ratchet
wrench—whatever helps
to hold back that surging
tide of stony, evil books.

This late winter after-
noon, come any flood,
after a hopeful respite
the waters of blood

toss over all sand, hat-
bands, flowered capes;
we are all always con-
scripted by our edges.

So rat me out, tell me
things I must never know.
Your feint of hands and
minds—ever slow, slow.

Grasshoppers intrude
far onto our workbench;
how can this, so weak,
be forceful all at once?

Rat me out you big- hearted Judas, send me
canny flowers, else—will I cave? Or cop a plea?

*The Open Gate* / R. J. Keeler

# Last Part: Literature

## Deception Pass

Like some odd, perhaps like
a singletary woman, tides
now resting against the pass
will, in the main, be slack at
night.

Yet the moon still rages strong
in my brain; and, like some cheap
woman, tides are at times neap,
at times slack, but in the main
at flood.

But may the dream compel the dreamer,
or may the dreamer ignore the dream?
And now the water dreams of its sea,
and cuneiforms drown at the pass's
feet.

The change from disorder to order
never slackens—enthusiasm bends
to failure, humility. Water's time
is not yet to act, but gravity's well is
number sixty-four.

Above—the clinging flame. Below—
the abysmal water. Thus, the book of
our future is beneath our feet, uncleft.
And—for Jung—a complete illness is
deep and just.

*The Open Gate* / R. J. Keeler

Firmland at the deep, dark bottom;
would Siddhartha fall for the pass's ruse?
A pebble on the lone beach is heard
to whisper, *This is no longer about loss—
or, about failings.*

## Chinese Gastronomy

"If one does not keep the cook in line,
he becomes insolent"
—Hsiang Ju Lin and Tsuifeng Lin, 1972

Star anise in brown sauce, chicken stock, soy sauce,
    brown sugar, whole cloves, ginger.
Steamed cucumber slivers, translucent; just before
    serving, lightly salted.
Green scallion pancakes; the scallions very finely
    chopped before adding.
Ingredients for the evening meal must be purchased
    that day, must be fresh.
Blanched mustard greens with oyster sauce poured
    over the shriveled leaves.
Happy family.


Glutinous rice. Corn starch blended into a white
    paste, added to firm up a dish.
Lightly poached trout covered in black beans soaked
    in wine and then crushed.
Steamed buns filled with pork or glutinous rice or
    sweet pudding or nuts.
Chinese gastronomy should strive to uncover
    essences but never overwhelm.
Wine vinegar out of the bottle
Fat purple eggplants, cut into long strips, fried in
black bean sauce and wine vinegar, a little sugar.


Fish cheeks delicately lifted from the steamed whole
    with fine carved ivory *kuàizi*, **c**hopsticks.
*Hsein*, a sweet natural flavor; it must always appear
    natural and effortless, present true essence.
Pearly meat balls: diced pork rolled in sticky rice,
    then steamed for an hour

Carnal pleasures.
Hot red pepper oil—finely diced red peppers inside a
 paper filter, smoking hot oil poured over.
It was the women who made life go on in these small
 villages.

Chicken wings simmered in brown sauce and star
 anise for hours and hours.
*Gastronomy*—the word suggests sensual indulgences.
Riches laid out on a far table—colors and scents,
rough and oily textures, steam from the kitchen.
The cooks in every region are like the secret tailors of
 cloth, of wedding dresses, luxurious cloaks.
Important to fold the dough over the sweet pork
 inside dumplings, then seal with a fork.

We had to learn how to eat before we could learn
 how to cook.

## The Point of Walking a Labyrinth

i.
Not going back in time, not adult history;
like a wax museum's clientele—upright, glaring.
Solomon stands on center, calculating, betting.
Who walks to right, to left, ahead, behind?
All shuffle at a same pace, more or less,
orderly and qualitative, alert as numb can be.
Situational awareness, sure, but why get all het up?
Shield, sword—defenses all sigh, *Fly high above*.
Else meet Asterion, who may just consume you
or send you back to first grade for heavy tutoring.
Regardless, the return path narrows wildly, tilled.


ii.
About a mind, how it folds on itself and turns
cochlea-like, even proboscis-like; the strongest swords
are hammered, folded over, then re-hammered.
Psychosis, hydra of convolutions—e.g., Hannah's color vision.
So take Thorazine, don't look back, save yourself;
Mandelbrot fractals simple by comparison.


iii.
Go, run ahead as quick as you choose. Don't
think a thing when you meet yourself, the older
or younger model. Nevertheless, you will not return,
never correct mistakes. Ignore blood spills along
this circular path—the spiral has its own rhythm.

iv.
Wanderlust a vein of silver rot
forced down a temperamental gullet.
Just keep leaning out to the left, step by step.
The crucible tightens up; moss grows on the
north side of the heart; nothing ends well—
"Abandon all hope. . ." and so on and so on.

# Alphabet

A sin to be obtuse, asleep, to not pay attention—so
    keep an observation log—life and thought.
Bend the pulse of gods and muse, make them thrum
    against your rusty letters.
Cut your own heart out, squeeze out your own blood,
    write in lines of song.
Desperate for immortal knowing? Search for Keats.
Euphrates, a twisted river, so like twisted rhymes;
    they're on their own, no recall.
From insanity and ugliness arise flowers of vividness,
    of literary hope, like those of Rimbaud.
Gout manifests in toes; ghazals manifest on paper,
    out of insanity and utter boredom.
*Honor the masters of the past.* Present-day masters
    nod and applaud, obey.
*Instantiation,* such an awkward word, but works of
    art instantiate elements of nature.
Just because language comes easy and naturally to
    you, no reason to torture yourself by writing.
Know excuses; get to work, open your heart, splay it
    out for glory.
Learn the basics—study the wildest writings you may
    uncover.
Master the obvious or rare forms: sonnet, crowns,
    syllabic, many others.
Never speculate about your own legend; go read what
    Merwin wrote about Berryman.
Orpheus wrote hexameter and pulled Euridice up
    from hell; go, do the same in your verse.
Pantoums, unless exquisite or very well-done, bore
    by the third stanza.
Quran's language described as *rhymed prose;* like a

good poem, easier to memorize.
Raskolnikov murdered for abstract ideas; WCW
    dictated, *No ideas but in things*.
Essence of great poetry? Genius, some say. Or luck.
    Or courage. Maybe wildness.
*Tangled web of lies*. Scott, not Shakespeare, but still
    an admirable objective for your long poems.
Ulysses, Odysseus, Homer, the *Odyssey*: please,
    write an epic poem about masts and sirens.
V. Perhaps it stands for *verse*, but also *voice*,
    *verisimilitude*, *vernacular*, or *vignette*.
Writers are born, work, die. One remarkable line;
    perhaps the only miracle you can hope for.
Excessively overworking your first draft? Likely
    turns it to mush. Better: deft restraint.
Why striving to get published? Why? Publishing is a
    form of extreme insanity.
Xanadu, Shangri-La. After decades of difficult,
    thankless work, may we find our way there.

# Amulet

Feldspar, clay, wood; brooch, charm, hook.
That lizard brain, amygdala, a wretched savant.
What the hell to do with small extremities—
a piece of bone from antelope, bear, or chinook?

The hidden forces of the universe
are unknown and invisible; old runes abide
deep under hot Kalahari sands
to ward off nectars of passion quite perverse.

Faith unwinds to bat away tense foils.
Paths to happy life—rub dead stones,
touch them each passage, they do jobs well.
Or scatter aged bones across temples' coils.

Our startling brains, how they work, if at all—
imagine earrings, passion plays, brilliant *Ariel.*

## Leverage
—After E. E. Cummings


festive presents come to whit
                             sunTide
at the                          merkele brothers
grocery
       and properl
y the whole packagegoesupwitha bang      !bang
           and leverage out from the cat
's feet kicking up
      into festive
      SILENCE ONto
          windowled
ges.     —sca(red by a little tric)k gif
           t which my   instantly   brother
sent—
       then
                      licks paw as if

    (nothing was ever the m,atter)   there at
merkele  's (d)ownto    w    n

[rat, !i'll get him] store. [back next ye(what?
puntpuntpuntnow!)ar just
like lucy to char.
(T.S!! brother)
      Liebraun]

## Blank Verses

I. After Shakespeare
Oh, Master, quite the stir your signal runs,
And leas't it harrows me, I come away.
Abundant quality your justice has,
To sup upon those most inclined to sin.
And thus we twist the badger in his sett,
So coax to ruin the feckless sanity
Of those in brotherhoods who hasten dark.

II. A Letter to Dr. Fred P. Brooks Jr.
The possibility of logging on
Decreases with each passing tick of time.
The Net is naught when massive files run,
And spread, and replicate—the overhead
Would stun the likes of you, Dr. Brooks,
But annoy Von Neumann twice as much.

So keep the boys and girls around the campus
And make them use the snail's painful mode.
Oh, keep their livelihood away from stocks
And make their only options faster webs,
That I might have a chance to check my funds
Before the market takes its final plunge.

Your friend in need of faster logging on.

## Trivial

> —*To make everything trivial, that is joy and wisdom. When everything is commonplace then nothing is important and hence painful.*

The clouds the sun the lost
the new. Once young the twister the broken
window the smell the camouflaged bug
death the writing blood on the road the
dirt the smell. Once young the fingernail
blue sky pushed the tip of the head through
the perineum yesterday this hour. Black
the wave of water the lost the wind
blowing leaves speculation blood on the
road caution the late traveler the shoe
the pinch the smell spring the noise of
bowels weapons joy the home. The right
foot once young estrus the shaking deep
in the earth joy Orion green grass this hour
excellence. A hundred years the faith consideration the twister food caution the latecomer
crushed spiders Ananias the plasma Wu the
lost art the rain time flies like an arrow.
Spirochete the one-hundred sixty-third
blue sky. Tree rings the fingernail the sun
compassion the sacred heart lessons.

## *Against the Fall of Night*
—Arthur C. Clarke, 1948

Tricks of honesty;
time's transits in hell.
Save us, forlorns cry.

Wonderments allow
carved spice bread,
wealthy godmothers,
accolades of light.

A workman knows his tools,
a waterman knows his crabs.
The waters of crucifixion,
like a woman beholden
at heavy gravity,
descend onto the moors.

Satan's lips divine:
lose the Hula-Hoop,
swim the marathon,
hack the protégée.

Heaven flags its sign.
Wildness at heart:
a fine lost token,
amulet.

## Both the Cross and Ecstasy of the Heart
—After Geoffrey Hill

Simple language points at April's truth,
at whether go the lambs of ancient hate,
barbarism. *Of course* we stove the heart;
the lance's tip alike the kind of Ruth.

Blood as water. Corpus's contagion
begets a sense of love, and coming loss.
A swell of pain and then, a look across,
and then, a second brief attenuation.

Peter denies; Sanhedrin priests deplore.
Green pastures anoint the Good Thief.
Some days roll by; Marcellus dons the cloth;
a weekend arrives; centurions off to whore.

The cross leans awkward and heavy.
Ecstasy drips in slowly very slowly.

## Disfluencies

"If you want to communicate, use a telephone."
– Richard Hugo

*Well, I guess, I don't know, really. I mean,
look, umm, why don't you know? Oh, that's—
that's what? What I mean is...uh.... Damn,
I forgot, forgot, forgot—what was it? What?
Well, you know, like I just forgot—well, you
know? I mean, you don't know? No? Great—
this is so silly, I wish—well, what more is there,
I mean, gosh. Let's see, now...see now.... Oh,
yes! Where was I? We were saying umm, gee.*

*What was it you were talking about? Yes, yes,
of course, it was—Oh, no it wasn't, was it? It was—
let me think a minute. You know, I think you're
right—the thing we were talking about? Oh, yes,
and.... What was it? But of course, that's it, it
was that, just that very thing, but, well, then, umm,
maybe it wasn't; or, it could have been, well, like....*

*Could that have been that? No, no, no, I don't
think so, but then, let's see, if it wasn't—what?
What was what? It must be something, might as
well be, it was word for word, I remember—of
course, by George, that's it! That's it!*

*Or, maybe, by and large, jeepers, jeez double-jeez,
it's so plain to me but...but let's see what you
think? That's, well, it's clear to me, you've
nailed it--lock, stock and barrel, my lips are,
umm, sealed, but there's the other thing, you know,
it's got to—go ahead, cut to the quick, to the*

*chase, man, let it out, let's have it now, or else!*


*You blankety-blank, you! Well, I never, what
do you know, I'd never have thought it of you,
so that's your game, well, we'll just see about
that, won't we now. You'll see! Hey! Wait a
minute! You have no right...well, maybe, OK,
you see--ack! Hmm, just a minute, I'll see,
perhaps—no, that's not it, just like, like this,
you know. Listen boys, old chap, shit fire, let's
go, come on now, don't make such a fuss. No
soap, nope, none at all, why you ask? Let it go,
now, leave well enough alone. It's over, all over,
pipe down, you-all, queue up, don't ask why, just
do it, let's be reasonable. Why, don't sass me, you—
you—you. Oh, what is it? So long, compadres,
stubborn as a mule, are you? Why, I'd sooner—no,
but I will. Uh, oh, uh-huh, uh, uh, huh? Y'know?
Willy-nilly. You-uns take care, now, like man,
do it, just do it! Like, ham!*

## God Among the Insects
*—1 Samuel, The Book of Ruth*

Attack with spears of sorts, with lance and sword,
and arrow—*not* defenseless before God.
All their rooming houses full of joy,
of spirit; children wild at parks, in alleys.

Now the realm of spirit, the honest hour.
Now everyone's a tenant, a visitor.
David, the second King of Israel,
constructs rainbows out of colored silk.

Tomorrow, week after, the uprising—
a transformation, metamorphosis.
God always carries chinks and frailties
sustained through fertility or pest of field.

David's fragile carapace insults.
Naomi will never die destitute.

*The Open Gate* / R. J. Keeler

## *Guerilla War,* The Libretto

Act Three, Scene 1
(A grassy plain near the jungle's edge.)

Señorita Tonya, with loaded chromed pistol

>The saying goes that timing's everything.
>The human body, when it works, it works
>so well; and once I tickled Che Guevara
>in his ribs—Bolivia, years
>ago. *The human species appears so strange—*
>*all bluff, deception, imbalance, great despair.*
>He dressed in camo, green and brown fatigues;
>a Luger in his belt, a bright whistle.
>He'd say, *The mind's a danger, deep in fear.*
>Always with the dark blue beret.

Father Aposto, her missionary confessor

>Unrest our consort; enemy's afraid.
>Diversity's a weapon; passion heals.
>Amid concerns, our sadness fuels our fight;
>my bended knee conceals my edgéd dagger.
>But winning is not our goal. Butterflies
>grumble about even the stinking moths.
>Was nothing off-limits or gentlemanly here?
>Separate cells, what defines each?

Chorus
>In hallways, in crossing, ever sure of breath.
>Holding the high pass against all.

# Holystone

Two years of waiting before a mast, then a turn:
a field of ripe poppies opens alongside that path
to push a storm eastward toward Bethlehem.
The manger is a holy relic—it can be traded;
will companions come or not to rescue the ass?

Back and forth, back and forth,
that's always like the task at hand.
No wonder we never get anywhere,
find ourselves back in same predicaments.

Thus, the intricate trickster coyote sails on:
*Safety, the middle of the pack; outliers get picked off.*
Turn to, swabbies, grind a teak deck down to white,
sear every veil off to real. The whole Jesus thing
a media cover-up, just like the moon landing.

Bury truth in enchanted blankets, let coyote loose to
rue.

## The Weld Is Always Stronger Than the Steel

A marriage of two sweet souls, that union
that buffers, befits, and protects, consents
amid songs or storms to true mutual assistance;
such fashion cements errants into high Eden.

When I was seven, I'd build balsam gliders
from boxed, store-bought parts. A clear cement,
*Duco* in a green foil tube, to glue spars to bent
ribs. On crash, glued joints held—ribs shattered.

But were that weld to be the weaker of the two,
to loosen its grip? Until friction or stress do us part—
an airplane wing or a sacred vow, both fall apart,
absent well-knit seams. So, *jamais vu* or *déjà vu*?

Go now, ask her, please go ask young Daphne:
*Peel your bark away from that lovely laurel tree.*

## Listen

An echo mixed within its own subtext
like a quiet whisper, or celestial music.
Silence arises not just alongside sound,

also within. So attend at every moment
to what's going on around you; every
word, spoken or not, has its very season

as it passes into discourse, raw or empty.
Say, *I have nothing else to say to you*!
Your heartbeat's adequate to this task.

A hawk's silence as it passes overhead,
the mouse's rustle in grass below. Who
can hear the sun in one ear and the sky

in the other? Or crisscross a lonely heart,
know its return echo? If you want
pages of dead manuscripts to murmur

to you—there's nothing there to be heard.
Shakespeare's breath a red demon in wait.

# Notes

- "A Ladder to Heaven": see 2 Chronicles 3:6, English Standard Version.
- "Blank Verses": Dr. Fred P. Brooks, Jr. was my MSCS thesis advisor at UNC-CH.
- *"Chinese Gastronomy"*: material from *Chinese Gastronomy* used with permission from Hastings House/Daytrips Publishers.
- "Corrosion and Its Many Uses": see "Hemoglobin," https://en.wikipedia.org/wiki/Hemoglobin
- "Deception Pass": material from Hexagram 64 of *The I Ching,* or *Book of Changes* used with permission from Princeton University Press.
- "Her Northern Sisters": see https://en.wikipedia.org/wiki/Ring_of_Fire
- "Men of Yesterday": see "Neanderthal-Denisovan Ancestors Interbred with a Distantly Related Hominin," *Science Advances* 6, no. 8 (Feb. 19, 2020): eaay5483.
- "Of Dual Nature: Chernobyl, after a Pause": Excerpts from https://www.britannica.com/science/radiation (specifically, https://www.britannica.com/science/radiation/Accumulation-in-critical-organs) and https://www.britannica.com/topic/Native-American (specifically, https://www.britannica.com/place/Arctic/Traditional-culture) are:
reprinted with permission from *Encyclopaedia Britannica*, © 2017 by Encyclopædia Britannica, Inc.

reprinted with permission from *Encyclopaedia Britannica*, © 2019 by Encyclopædia Britannica, Inc.
- "On First Looking into Perelman's Proof of Poincaré's Conjecture": see Grisha Perelman, "The Entropy Formula for the Ricci Flow and Its Geometric Applications," arXiv:math/0211159, arXivLabs, Cornell University, https://arxiv.org/abs/math/0211159; Donald O'Shea, *The Poincaré Conjecture: In Search of the Shape of the Universe*; W. A. Graham, *The Custer Myth*; and Andrew Motion, *Keats: A Biography*.
- "Q-Boats": see "Q-ship," https://tinyurl.com/13zfxiy1; and "Q-ship," https://en.wikipedia.org/wiki/Q-ship. See also "Quisling," https://en.wikipedia.org/wiki/Quisling
- "Ruin as Gift, or The Equations of the Science of Love": see "Newton's Laws of Motion," https://en.wikipedia.org/wiki/Newton%27s_laws_of_motion; "Maxwell's Equations," https://en.wikipedia.org/wiki/Maxwell%27s_equations; and "Mass–Energy Equivalence," https://en.wikipedia.org/wiki/Mass%E2%80%93energy_
- "Rune": see "Pick a Rune and Discover Its Message for You," *Conscious Reminder*, https://consciousreminder.com/2017/05/08/pick-a-rune-to-discover-its-message/
- "Sin-Eaters": see "Sin-Eater," https://en.wikipedia.org/wiki/Sin-eater; and Domagoj Valjak, "The Macabre Story of Sin-Eaters,"

https://www.thevintagenews.com/2018/08/06/sin-eaters/
- "The Bodhisattva on the Ballard Bridge": see "At Large in Ballard: Crossing the Bridge," *Westside Seattle*, June 7, 2010, https://www.westsideseattle.com/robinson-papers/2010/06/07/large-ballard-crossing-bridge; and also "Meet Me at The Sorrento," *Seattle PI*, June 8, 2010, https://blog.seattlepi.com/ballard/2010/06/08/meet-me-at-the-sorrento/
- "The Dinosaurs Went Extinct Because They Didn't Have a Space Program": see Jonathan Amos, "Dinosaur Asteroid Hit 'Worst Possible Place,'" BBC News, May 15, 2017, https://www.bbc.com/news/science-environment-39922998

# About the Author

R. J. (Robert) Keeler was born in St. Paul, Minnesota, and grew up in the jungles of Colombia. He holds a BA in Mathematics from North Carolina State University, an MS in Computer Science from the University of North Carolina-Chapel Hill, an MBA from UCLA, and a Certificate in Poetry from the University of Washington.

He was an Honorman in the US Naval Submarine School and was Submarine Service (SS) qualified. He received the Vietnam Service Medal, and an Honorable Discharge. He also received a Whiting Foundation Experimental Grant.

Keeler is a member of IEEE (technological society), AAAS (scientific society), and the Academy of American Poets. He is also a former Boeing engineer.

Keeler currently lives on Vashon Island, Washington. He is a minor Luddite, thus can only be contacted by email at *open_gate@alumni.ucla.edu*.

*The Open Gate* is his third published book of poetry. His first was *Detonation* (Wipf and Stock, 2020) and his second was *Snowman* (Manor House, 2020).

Manor House
905-648-4797
www.manor-house-publishing.com

www.ingramcontent.com/pod-product-compliance
Lightning Source LLC
LaVergne TN
LVHW011951070526
838202LV00054B/4899